There are hundreds
and hundreds of reasons
why this book had to
be written – turn
to the back to see
just a few . . .

Subject

The subject is the person or thing doing the action.

① Find the verb.

② Ask yourself, who or what is doing the verb?

Jasper ran to school.
ran is the verb.
Who or what ran? Jasper ran.
So – Jasper is the subject.

The car drove away from school.
drove is the verb.
Who or what drove? The car drove.
So – The car is the subject.

Object

The object is the person or thing having the action done to them.

① Find the verb.

② Ask yourself, who or what is having something done to them?

Joseph is riding the bike.
riding is the verb.
Who or what was ridden? The bike was ridden.
So – the bike is the object.

I love you.
love is the verb.
Who is loved? You are loved.
So – you are the object.

Main Clause

A main clause is usually a complete sentence.

It has a subject and an object.

It makes sense on its own.

Scarlett likes dogs but not cats.

Scarlett likes dogs (main clause)

Connie continued to write even though it was late.

Connie continued to write (main clause)

Subordinate Clause

A subordinate clause is not a complete sentence.

It needs a main clause.

It does not make sense on its own.

Scarlett likes dogs but not cats.

but not cats (subordinate clause)

Connie continued to write even though it was late.

even though it was late (subordinate clause)

Active Voice

The active voice means that the subject of the sentence is doing the action.

Geo is eating the potato.

Geo is the subject and he is **eating** the potato.
(active voice)

Aurelie and Holly are watching the birds.

Aurelie and Holly are the subject and they are **watching** the birds.
(active voice)

Passive Voice

The passive voice means that the subject of the sentence is having something done to it.

The potato is being eaten by Geo.

The potato is the subject and it is being **eaten** by Geo. (passive voice)

The birds are being watched by Aurelie and Holly.

The birds are the subject and they are being **watched** by Aurelie and Holly. (passive voice)

Formal Language / Informal Language

Formal language uses full sentences with the correct grammar and punctuation.

It does not use contractions.

It is not possible to go out at the moment because it is raining hard.

Informal language is casual and is used when talking or writing to family or friends.

Contractions and abbreviations can be used.

I can't go out now 'cos it's chucking it down.

Phrase

A phrase is a group of words that go together to add meaning.

A phrase is not a complete sentence.

A phrase is added to a sentence to make it more interesting.

A phrase does not have a subject and a verb.

Hattie walks home. (no phrase)

My friend Hattie walks home. (one phrase)

My friend Hattie walks home after school.
(two phrases)

Contractions

The apostrophe shows where the letters have been left out.

I am	=	I'm
you are	=	you're
he would	=	he'd
we had	=	we'd
they have	=	they've
they will	=	they'll
have not	=	haven't
should have	=	should've

Two words are now one word.

Apostrophe Possession

Singular (to show ownership)

Emma's dress ⎫ Only one Emma,
The baker's shop ⎬ one baker and
The dog's bowl ⎭ one dog

Plural (to show more than one owner)

The boys' cloakroom ⎫ Lots of boys,
Pets' corner ⎬ pets and birds
Birds' nests ⎭

Irregular ones (the whole word changes)

The ladies' hairdresser ⎫ These words
The children's playground ⎬ already show more
The policemen's radios ⎭ than one owner

Inverted Commas

Use double inverted commas for speech.

(speech marks)

"Henry and Sam will be here soon,"
said IslaJane.

Inverted commas for speech always go outside any other punctuation.

"Can we have biscuits and hot chocolate?"
asked Alex.

Use single inverted commas for quotations.

(quote marks)

Inverted commas for quotations only go round the actual quote.

'Sleep that knits up the ravell'd sleeve of care',
Shakespeare.

Inverted commas can sometimes be used to indicate a special meaning such as irony or sarcasm.

That looks 'delicious'.

Direct Speech / Indirect Speech

Direct Speech

"Have you finished your homework, Bonnie?"
asked her mother.

These are the exact words spoken by
Bonnie's mother.

Direct speech always needs inverted commas.
(speech marks)

Indirect Speech or Reported Speech

Bonnie's mother asked her if she had finished
her homework.

These are not the exact words used by
Bonnie's mother.

They do not need inverted commas.
(speech marks)

Commas

A comma marks a brief pause to help make sense of what is written.

- To separate words or phrases at the beginning of a sentence.

    Yes, you are in the team.

- To separate words or phrases at the end of a sentence.

    Can Ethni come over to play, please?

- Lists.

    We bought grapes, bananas, pineapple and oranges.

- Terms of address.

    Milo, time to go now.

- In an address.

    They used to live at Via Woronoff 24, Grimaldi Superiore, Italy.

Commas

And also …

- To separate extra information in a sentence.

  Harry, who is a lawyer, lives abroad.

- To separate a subordinate clause.

Although the cake was huge, they managed to
eat it all.

- To separate conjunctive adverbs.

  Suddenly, the phone rang; astonishingly,
  it was an old friend.

- Direct Speech.

  "I scored two goals," shouted James.

  "I'll be back soon," whispered Django,
  "just you wait and see."

Colons / Semicolons

A colon points ahead to something that follows.

It could be a list or to summarise or to explain.

Charlie is going to buy four things: butter, sugar, eggs and flour.

Finn ran off: he must have seen a rabbit.

A semicolon joins two sentences that are closely linked, perhaps where a full stop is too much and a comma is not enough.

George played very well yesterday; he broke his own record.

A semicolon can also be used to show a sharp contrast.

My sister hates dancing; I love it.

Full Stop / Exclamation Mark / Question Mark

A full stop is used at the end of a sentence.

The sun was out and the sky was blue.

A full stop is used to separate initials.

E. S. B. Tyrrell

An exclamation mark is used at the end of a short command.

Quick! Let's go!

An exclamation mark is also used to show emotion.

What an absolutely beautiful day!

A question mark is used to indicate a question.

"Can you come to my party?"

Statement / Command / Question

A statement tells you something in a clear and definite way and ends with a full stop.

Remi ran up the hill.

A command is an order to do something and ends with an exclamation mark.

Remi, run!

A question needs an answer and ends with a question mark.

Who is running?

Root Words

The root is the basic word to which a prefix or a suffix can be added.

impolite (a prefix has been added)

jumped (a suffix has been added)

uncomfortable (a prefix and a suffix have been added)

Prefix / Suffix

A prefix comes before a word to change its meaning.

un   im   in   non   mis   ir   il ...

unreal   disappear   impossible

A suffix comes after a word to change its meaning.

ing   able   ful   ish   ed

played   dreaming   astonishment

- It is possible that the un prefix was created by Shakespeare because he was the first to use it in print and on the stage.

Alliteration

Alliteration is the repetition of the beginning sound of several words in a sentence.

short sharp shock

singing softly

ruby red rose

deep dark dimples

Synonym / Antonym

Synonyms have the same meaning.

huge - colossal

ancient - old

option - choice

Antonyms have the opposite meaning.

start - finish

buy - sell

junior - senior

Homophones / Compound Words

Homophones are words that sound the same but are different in spelling and meaning.

son - sun

knot - not

aloud - allowed

Compound words are two separate words that are joined together to make one complete word.

snow + flake = snowflake

pan + cake = pancake

birth + day = birthday

Similes / Metaphors

A simile is a comparison using as or like.

... as happy as a lark.

... like a bolt of lightning.

A metaphor only hints at a comparison.

You're a star.

Georgina is a mine of information.

Personification / Onomatopoeia

Use personification to describe an inanimate object as if it were alive.

The dappled shadows played on the ceiling above my bed.

The sun smiled back at me as I pulled open the curtains.

Use onomatopoeia if you want a word that sounds like its meaning.

sizzle   crackle   ooze

Parenthesis / Dash

Parentheses are brackets used for extra information or explanation.

Crockham Hill (in Kent) is a lovely place to live.

A dash can be used for the same purpose.

Crockham Hill - that lovely, lovely little village - is in Kent.

Dashes can also be used for interruption or repetition.

"I wonder if - "

"Pl - pl - please may I have another one," pleaded her friend.

Hyphen

A hyphen is used to join prefixes or words
to make clear the meaning of the sentence.

I am going to recover. (means to get well)

I am going to re-cover my old exercise book.
(means to stick on a new cover)

Twenty five-kilometre runs
Twenty-five kilometre runs
Twenty-five-kilometre runs

(all mean something different)

Ellipsis

An ellipsis is a row of three dots.

An ellipsis is used to mark a pause, or to create suspense, at the end of a sentence.

Imogen took hold of the box with both hands, carefully lifted the lid, and slowly . . .

An ellipsis is also used to indicate a pause in speech.

"Thank you so much, Josie . . . it's absolutely lovely."

Bullet Points

Bullet points are used to make it easy to read a vertical list.

When I go to London I want to:

- Watch the Changing of the Guard.

- Look up at Nelson's Column.

- Walk over the Millennium Bridge.

- Have tea in a fancy hotel.

- Visit the Tower of London.

Determiners

Determiners are used before a noun
or a noun phrase.

a an the	articles
this that these	demonstratives
his my their	possessives
some each a few	quantifiers
one two three	numbers
first second last	ordinals

Articles

An article is always used with a noun.

The is the definite article and is used to refer to something specific.

    The gorilla (meaning a particular one)

A, an are indefinite articles which are used to refer to one of several.

    A chimpanzee (meaning one of several)
    An orangutan (meaning one of several)

A is used before words which sound as if they start with a consonant.

    a book   a pencil   a unicorn

An is used before words which sound as if they start with a vowel.

    an apple   an umbrella   an heir

Nouns

A noun is a naming word.

Proper nouns name people and places and always begin with a capital letter.

Sunday   Christmas   Daisyella

Common nouns name things that you can see, hear, touch or smell.

book   mango   train

Abstract nouns name ideas and feelings.

happiness   freedom   honesty

Collective nouns name collections.

swarm   forest   crowd

A noun phrase is made up of a noun and other words that go with it.

The little red guitar

Noun Phrase / Extended Noun Phrase

A noun phrase is made up of a noun and a few words to describe it.

The birthday cake.
(noun)

An extended noun phrase is made up of a noun and several words to describe it.

The most deliciously rich, dark chocolate birthday cake.
(noun)

Adjectives

An adjective describes a noun.

A deep river   The baby looked happy

Interrogative adjectives ask a question about a noun.

Which one would you like?

Demonstrative adjectives answer the question.

These cakes and those pastries look delicious.

Possessive adjectives or determiners show ownership and are used before a noun.

This is my dog.

Adjectives of quantity answer the question - How much?

The four children packed lots of food in the box until it was too heavy to carry.

Comparison of adjectives.

one	two	more than two
big	bigger	biggest
beautiful	more beautiful	most beautiful

Pronouns

Pronouns replace a noun.

Jacob caught the ball.
He   caught   it

Singular pronouns refer to one person or thing.

you   me   him

Plural pronouns refer to more that one.

them   us   we

Possessive pronouns refer to ownership.

mine   ours   their

Relative pronouns link two clauses together.

who   which   that

Use who for people.
Use which for things.
Use that for people and things.

Page 34

Verbs

A verb is a being or doing word.
A verb describes action or a state of being.

eat   dream   feel   sing   do . . .

Rosie ran across the grass and jumped into her mother's arms.

An auxiliary verb is more than one word.
It helps out the main verb and can also help to form tenses.

I have eaten   I am sleeping   We are sailing

Jazzy is going to the party.
Jazzy has arrived at the party.

Modal Verbs

Modal verbs suggest ability, possibility, permission, obligation or advice.

Modal verbs can be used alone or alongside a main verb.

Mia should pass the test.

should is the modal verb.
pass is the main verb.

could   may   can   might   must   ought to
shall   should   will   would   have to

He can jump over the stream. - ability
She might arrive today.   - possibility
May I borrow your book?   - permission
We have to go now.   - obligation
You should try again.   - advice

Adverbs

Adverbs describe verbs.

immediately   politely   joyfully

Adverbs can also describe adjectives and other adverbs.

Hamish runs swiftly

- tells you more about the verb.

Hamish runs very swiftly

- tells you more about another adverb.

Hamish is unbelievably swift

- tells you more about the adjective.

Adverbials

An adverbial is a word or phrase, which is used like an adverb.

An adverbial adds extra information to a sentence.

An adverbial explains how, when and where.

Adverbials can be used in different parts of a sentence.

All day long Ayuni played on the beach.
(beginning of the sentence)

Ayuni played on the beach all day long.
(end of the sentence)

Ayuni played happily on the beach.
(after the verb)

Ayuni often played on the beach.
(before the verb)

Fronted adverbials

A fronted adverbial has been moved to the front or the beginning of the sentence.

A fronted adverbial adds more information to the rest of the sentence.

Before anyone was awake, **Anna tiptoed downstairs.**

More fronted adverbials.

Soon, Last Tuesday, After a while
- tell you more about time
Once again, Daily, Never
- tell you more about frequency
Nearby, In the distance, Outside
- tell you more about place
Without a word, Unexpectedly, Happily
- tell you more about manner
Out of breath, Maybe, Somewhat overawed
- tell you more about possibility

Conjunctions or Connectives / Prepositions

Conjunctions or connectives are used to join two short sentences to make one longer one.

and but although until since before as …

Sophia was smiling. She had passed her exam.

Sophia was smiling because she had passed her exam.

Prepositions show the relationship between one thing and another usually indicating time or place.

during outside above after against beneath …

Immy dived into the pool.

Parts of Speech - Summary

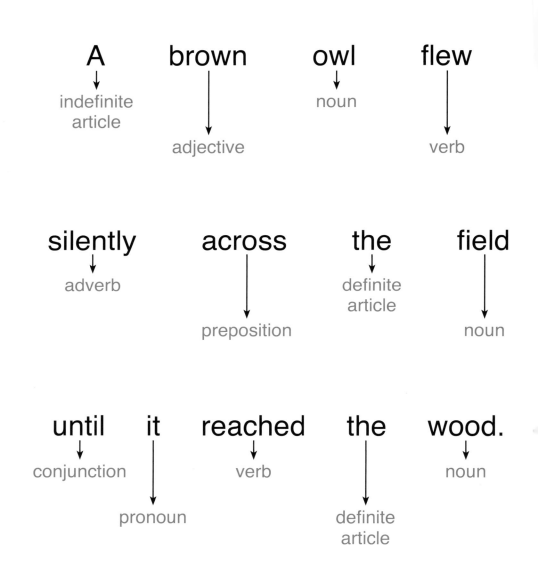

A — indefinite article

brown — adjective

owl — noun

flew — verb

silently — adverb

across — preposition

the — definite article

field — noun

until — conjunction

it — pronoun

reached — verb

the — definite article

wood. — noun

Tenses

Past	Present	Future
(yesterday)	(today)	(tomorrow)
I ran	I run	I will run
I went	I go	I may go
I ate	I eat	I shall eat
I dug	I dig	I will dig

An easy way to remember is that:

The past is yesterday.

The present is today.

The future is tomorrow.

Present Progressive

The present progressive tense is used to show that something is going on now.

The present progressive tense is also used to indicate that there is a future planned activity.

am   is   are

Use am, is or are before a verb ending in ing.

I am going

She is staying

They are laughing

Also available:

Mrs J Rules
Warning
May make maths seem easy!

Mrs J Rocks
Warning
May make English seem easy!

Mrs J @ Home
Warning
May make teaching your own children easy!

Mrs J's Brilliant Tables Game
Warning
May make tables learning easy!

The College Collection
Stories for dyslexic or reluctant readers aged 9-13yrs.
Crown House Publishing.

Contents

Subject.. 1

Object 2

Main Clause... 3

Subordinate Clause 4

Active Voice.. 5

Passive Voice 6

Formal Language 7

Informal Language................................. 7

Phrase 8

Contractions 9

Apostrophe Possession........................ 10

Inverted Commas 11

Direct Speech 12

Indirect Speech.................................... 12

Commas .... 13 &14

Colons 15

Semicolons 15

Full Stop 16

Exclamation Mark................................. 16

Question Mark...................................... 16

Statement 17

Command 17

Question 17

Root Words... 18

Prefix 19

Suffix... 19

Alliteration... 20

Synonym.. 21

Antonym 21

Homophones 22

Compound Words.. 22
Simile... 23
Metaphor 23
Personification 24
Onomatopoeia.. 24
Parenthesis... 25
Dash 25
Hyphen 26
Ellipsis 27
Bullet Points.. 28
Determiners 29
Articles.. 30
Nouns 31
Noun Phrase.. 32
Extended Noun Phrase 32
Adjectives 33
Comparison of Adjectives 33
Pronouns 34
Verbs 35
Auxiliary Verb... 35
Modal Verb 36
Adverbs 37
Adverbials... 38
Fronted Adverbials... 39
Conjunctions/Connectives...................................... 40
Prepositions... 40
Parts of Speech, Summary...................................... 41
Past, Present, Future Tense 42
Present Progressive Tense...................................... 43

Here they are!

Also -

Many thanks to H and Dj for their endless encouragement and all those who helped with proof reading.

If you found this book useful and would like a few more copies for friends and family
Email: mrsjrules@hotmail.co.uk
Or go to: mrsj.edenkent.org